PAC-MAN:

ARCADE PIONEER

x1980

Kenny Abdo

Fly!
An Imprint of Abdo Zoom
abdobooks.com

abdobooks.com

Published by Abdo Zoom, a division of ABDO, P.O. Box 398166, Minneapolis, Minnesota 55439. Copyright © 2022 by Abdo Consulting Group, Inc. International copyrights reserved in all countries. No part of this book may be reproduced in any form without written permission from the publisher. Fly!™ is a trademark and logo of Abdo Zoom.

Printed in the United States of America, North Mankato, Minnesota.
102021
012022

THIS BOOK CONTAINS RECYCLED MATERIALS

Photo Credits: Alamy, AP Images, Everett Collection, flickr, Getty Images, Shutterstock, ©AntMan3001 p.cover / CC BY-SA 2.0, ©Marica Massaro p.6 /CC BY-SA 4.0, ©Chris Pirillo p.16 / CC BY-NC-ND 2.0
Production Contributors: Kenny Abdo, Jennie Forsberg, Grace Hansen
Design Contributors: Candice Keimig, Neil Klinepier

Library of Congress Control Number: 2021940179

Publisher's Cataloging-in-Publication Data

Names: Abdo, Kenny, author.
Title: Pac-Man: arcade pioneer / by Kenny Abdo
Other Title: arcade pioneer
Description: Minneapolis, Minnesota : Abdo Zoom, 2022 | Series: Video game heroes |
    Includes online resources and index.
Identifiers: ISBN 9781098226961 (lib. bdg.) | ISBN 9781644947418 (pbk.) |
    ISBN 9781098227807 (ebook) | ISBN 9781098228224 (Read-to-Me ebook)
Subjects: LCSH: Video game characters--Juvenile literature. | Pac-Man (Game)-
    Juvenile literature. | Video game arcades--Juvenile literature. | Heroes--Juvenile
    literature.
Classification: DDC 794.8--dc23

TABLE OF CONTENTS

PAC-MAN

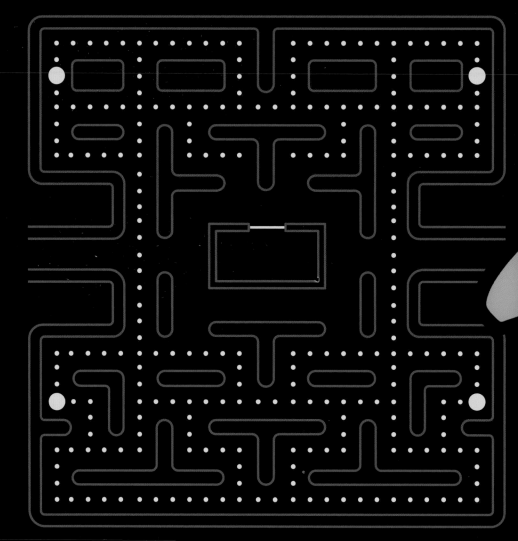

Cruising through mazes, eating fruit, and busting ghosts is all in a day's work for Pac-Man.

Featured on cereal boxes, the cover of *Time* magazine, and cartoon shows, Pac-Man is the most recognizable character in video game history!

PLAYER PROFILE

Toru Iwatani was just 22 years old when he began work at video game **developing** company Namco. He had no interest in designing video games. Iwatani wanted to work on pinball machines.

Iwatani had an idea based on the words *paku paku*, meaning "chomping" in Japanese. The concept became a game called *Puckman*. Eventually, Namco founder Masaya Nakamura changed it to *Pac-Man*.

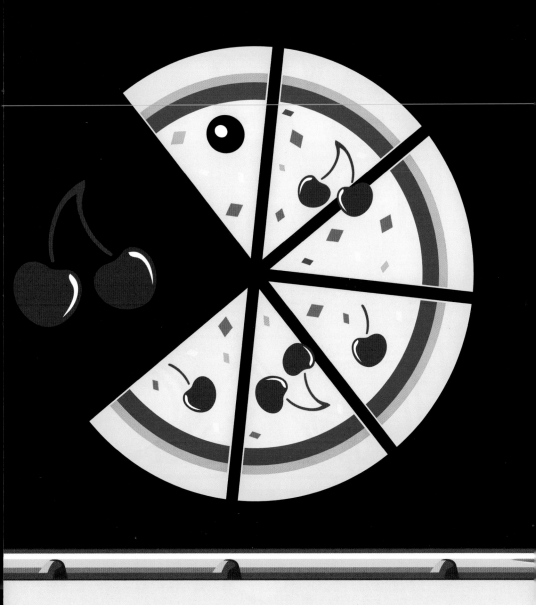

Pac-Man was brought to life by just a few people. Shigeo Funaki **programmed** while Toshio Kai did sound and music. Iwatani, inspired by a pizza missing a slice, designed the character.

LEVEL UP

The first *Pac-Man* machine was installed in a Tokyo movie theater in 1980. The company sold 350,000 machines within 18 months! *Pac-Man* was a worldwide sensation.

The success of *Pac-Man* inspired many **sequels**. *Professor Pac-Man*, *Pac-Man Plus*, *Baby Pac-Man*, and *Ms. Pac-Man* were just a few.

Ms. Pac-Man is considered the best of the series by fans. Ms. Pac-Man was the first playable female character in any game. She paved the way for characters like Samus Aran.

Toru Iwatani returned to *Pac-Man* in 2007 with *Pac-Man Championship Edition*. The game wowed fans with crazier time limits and transforming maze **layouts**.

Pac-Man 99 hit the Nintendo Switch in 2021. The **battle royale** style game allowed up to 99 players to compete at the same time. The game was an instant success!

EXPANSION PACK

Pac-Man got his own cartoon series in 1982. He also appeared as a playable character in many other games, including *Mario Kart Arcade GP* and *Street Fighter x Tekken*.

Guinness World Records recognizes that more than 293,000 *Pac-Man* machines were installed worldwide between 1981 and 1987. The game has been played an estimated 10 billion times.

For a character who was based off a pizza, Pac-Man is more than just a slice of history. He's the whole pie.

GLOSSARY

arcade – an indoor space that has multiple video games to play.

Battle Royale – a competition between many participants that goes until there is only one player left.

developer – a company that builds and creates software and video games.

layout – the way video games and their levels are arranged for play.

program – to create coded instructions for performances in video games.

sequel – a video game that continues the story begun in a preceding one.

ONLINE RESOURCES

Booklinks
NONFICTION NETWORK
FREE! ONLINE NONFICTION RESOURCES

To learn more about Pac-Man, please visit abdobooklinks.com or scan this QR code. These links are routinely monitored and updated to provide the most current information available.

INDEX